GW00361544

Compilation copyright © 1997 Lion Publishing
This edition copyright © 1997 Lion Publishing
Text copyright © 1997 Tom Wright
The author asserts the moral right to be
identified as the author of this work

Published by
Lion Publishing plc
Sandy Lane West, Oxford, England
ISBN 0 7459 3840 X
First edition 1997
10 9 8 7 6 5 4 3 2 1 0
A catalogue record for this book is
available from the British Library
Printed and bound in Singapore

Commissioning editor: Meryl Doney
Project editor: Nina Webley
Book designer: Jonathan Roberts
Jaket designer: Jonathan Robers
Studio photography: Andrew Whittuck

A Moment of

Celebration

Tom Wright

LION
Giftlines

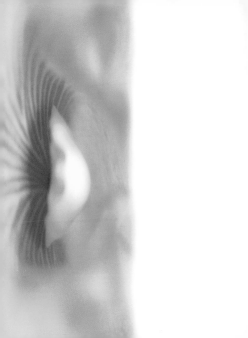

Contents

Introduction

These books are designed to help you explore the presence of God. You can open them at random. Or you can work through, perhaps, a page a day.

The books move in a sequence. The first, *A Moment of Prayer*, starts at the centre, and looks at the words of prayer. The second, *A Moment of Quiet*, explores what happens when we stop talking and listen. The third, *A Moment of Peace*, is about reconciliation between God and ourselves. The final volume, *A Moment of Celebration*, is about worshipping God, alone or with others.

Everybody celebrates sometimes. The trick is to do it in the presence of God. That's why Christians have developed liturgy (written forms of public worship), turning celebration into an art form. That's why, too, we use our bodies in worship, acting out the truth we're celebrating.

The high point of Christian celebration is the Eucharist (the word means 'thanksgiving'). As we follow Jesus' example, and obey his command, sharing bread and wine in his name, we enjoy a fellowship with Jesus and with one another that goes beyond words.

This book is designed to help you get the best out of all your celebrations of God's goodness.

'Come, let us worship and fall
down and kneel before the
Lord our maker.'

Worship
is...

$Worship$ is...
glimpsing
the beauty
of God,
and stopping
to gaze in
wonder.

Worship is...
sensing the
love of God,
        and opening up to it
    like a flower
in the sunshine.

Worship is...
believing in God's victory over
   evil
         and death,
   and
         celebrating it.

Worship
is . . .
thanking
God for sending
Jesus.

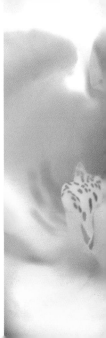

Worship
is . . .
celebrating the
presence and
power of God's
Spirit.

We

pray

together

We pray together...

because when I want to

sing to God but I'm not

sure of the tune, it helps

if I'm standing next to

others who know it.

We pray together...

because, while improvising

music is wonderful, producing it

together means you have to

agree on the speed and

harmony.

We pray together...

because when I use someone

else's prayer I realize it's the

prayer I wanted to pray but

didn't know how.

We pray together...
because when you're not a very
strong swimmer, or when you're
tired, or not sure which way to
swim, you'll do better to float in
a strong river than to thrash
around in a pond.

We pray together...

because when you're learning to

play an instrument, it's more

fun to play in an orchestra than

to tootle away all by yourself.

We worship
together...
because if my candle is to
stay alight, it helps if it's
in a line of other candles,
and in a place where the
fire has descended before.

We worship together...
as an act of faith,
opening our eyes to
God's dimension of
reality and joining in the
worship of the angels,
the saints and the whole
of creation.

We worship together...
as an act of hope,
because God's new
world will be a place
of worship, and our
worship here is like a
choir practice for the
real thing.

We worship together...

as an act of love,

since my sisters and

brothers need me as

 much as

I need them.

We worship

together...

as an act of humility,

abandoning our

arrogant isolation and

self-sufficiency.

Liturgy

Liturgy is...
the dance of God,
in which by his
Spirit we learn the
measure of his
love.

Liturgy is...

how we retain our grasp on the

Bible and the truth of God,

even when no one is teaching

us very much.

Liturgy is . . .

the rhythm of God's grace and

my acceptance of it, teaching

me the gospel through the

drama we act out.

Liturgy is...
God's means of
linking us to his
deeds in the past,
and making us the
preparation for what
he is going to do next.

Liturgy is...
a place we can feel
at home, where
we know where
everything is and
how everything
works.

Liturgy is...
the suit of clothes we
know we are
comfortable in.

Liturgy is...
the way we tell the
story of God, his
world and his people
—always the same,
yet with infinite
variations.

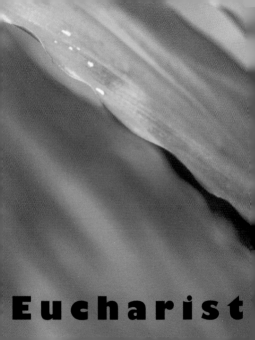

Eucharist

Eucharist

is...

where

belief

becomes

taste.

Eucharist

is...

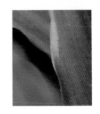

where

we gently

close our fingers

on to

hope.

Eucharist

is...

where

God beyond us

meets

God within us.

Eucharist is...

where love

meets love.

Eucharist is...

the engagement

party,

as we wait

for the marriage

supper of the Lamb.

Eucharist is...
the Christian
Passover, reminding
us that we are God's
free children and that
soon the whole
creation will be free
as well.

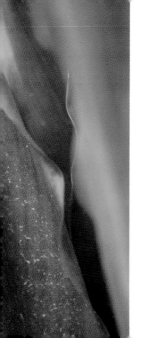

Eucharist is...

God saying

to us what he

said in Jesus:

'This is my

body, given

for you.'

Eucharist is...
God saying to us what he said
to Jesus: 'You are my beloved
child, with you I am well
pleased.'

E u c h a r i s t   i s . . .
*God saying to us what he said
through Jesus: 'Go, and
announce the Kingdom of God.'*

Eucharist is...
where we can
celebrate without
being silly, and
grieve without
being
depressed.

Eucharist is...
where we can ask
unanswerable
questions without
getting frustrated,
and express our
love without
being sentimental.

We celebrate the Eucharist

We celebrate the Eucharist...
because lovers need to have a
place and a time where they
know they can rely on each
other to be.

We celebrate

the Eucharist...

because a family

isn't a family

unless it sits down

at table together.

We celebrate

the Eucharist...

because you learn

to eat and drink

before you learn

to walk and talk.

*We celebrate
the Eucharist...
because at the end, all
creation will be flooded with
God's presence, and here we
glimpse this in advance in
bread and wine.*

We celebrate
the Eucharist...
because when we learn to
recognize Jesus in the
Eucharist, we also learn to
see him homeless on the
street.

Blessings

'Rejoice in the Lord always!
Again I say, rejoice! And the
peace of God, which passes all
understanding, will guard your
hearts and minds in
Christ Jesus.'

Jesus said: 'Those who eat my flesh and drink my blood have eternal life; and I will raise them up on the last day.'